Scientists Who Made History

Galileo GALILEI

Dr Mike Goldsmith

an imprint of Hodder Children's Books

Produced for Hodder Wayland by
White-Thomson Publishing Ltd
2/3 St Andrew's Place
Lewes
BN7 1UP

Editor: Polly Goodman
Designer: Derek Lee
Picture Researcher: Shelley Noronha, Glass Onion Pictures
Cover and Title Page Illustrator: Richard Hook
Science Panel Illustrator: Derek Lee
Consultant: Dr Brian Bowers, Senior Research Fellow at the Science Museum, London.

Published in Great Britain in 2001 by Hodder Wayland, an imprint of Hodder Children's Books.

British Library Cataloguing in Publication Data
Goldsmith, Mike (Scientists Who Made History)
1.Galilei, Galileo, 1564–1642 – Juvenile literature
2. Astronomers – Italy – Biography – Juvenile literature
3. Scientists – Italy – Biography – Juvenile literature
I. Title
520.9'2

ISBN 0 7502 3447 4

Printed and bound in Italy by G. Canale & C.S.p.A, Turin

Hodder Children's Books
A division of Hodder Headline Limited
338 Euston Road, London, NW1 3BH

Picture Acknowledgements: Bridgeman Art Library 4, 7, 13, 16, 20, 21, 31, 37; Corbis 5, 6 (bottom), 10, 11, 15, 19, 23, 25, 32, 33 (bottom), 39, 40, 43; Hodder Wayland Picture Library 33 (top), 38; Mary Evans Picture Library 6 (top), 9, 17, 28, 30, 36; Peter Newark 18; Science Photo Library 12, 24, 27 (bottom), 29, 35; Science and Society 22, 26, 27 (top), 34, 41, 42; Scala 14.

Contents

Daring to Challenge

IN THEIR OWN WORDS

'I think that in discussions of physical problems, we ought to begin not from the authority of scriptural passages [religious writing], but from sense-experiences and necessary demonstrations.'

GALILEO, WRITING ABOUT THE IMPORTANCE OF OBSERVATION AND EXPERIMENT, IN 1615.

THE THREE MEN reached the top of the Leaning Tower of Pisa at last and paused to catch their breath after their long climb. Silently, they strode to the edge of the tower and looked down at the crowd clustered 54 metres below. The crowd had been talking, but silence fell as they saw that Galileo Galilei, the man who had dared to challenge the ancient wisdom, had arrived. In a few seconds everyone would see who was right – the great thinkers of the past, or this young upstart.

At the top of the tower, Galileo gestured his two assistants forward. One of the men held a small metal sphere, weighing less than a kilogram. The other carried a sphere that weighed twenty times as much. Together the men held their spheres out over the parapet of the tower.

The physics of Aristotle, the ancient Greek philospher, predicted that the lighter sphere would fall twenty times slower than the heavier one, taking twenty times as long to reach the ground. And Aristotle could not be wrong. It was unthinkable to most people at this time.

LEFT: *This portrait of Galileo was painted in 1636, when he was seventy-two. Even at this age, Galileo was still developing new scientific theories.*

Galileo paused, enjoying the moment. He had no doubt about what would happen. Years of observation and experiment had taught him that Aristotle was hopelessly wrong. But what was obvious to him was almost blasphemous to his teachers.

The moment had come. Galileo gestured, and his assistants dropped their spheres. Three seconds later, both hit the ground at the foot of the tower – almost together. The mutter from the crowd which drifted faintly up to Galileo marked the beginning of a new method of thinking, a method based on observation and experiment – the method of modern science.

ABOVE: *A US astronaut from the* Apollo 15 *space mission on the Moon in 1972. More than three centuries after Galileo first studied the Moon through a telescope, human beings landed there.*

LEFT: *This 18th-century engraving shows people being led to the stakes to be burnt alive for questioning the authority of the Catholic Church.*

BELOW: *A statue of the ancient Greek thinker Aristotle. His influence held back the progress of physics for thousands of years.*

Galileo's world

The world that Galileo grew up in was very different to our own. In the sixteenth century, everyone thought that the ancient Greek philosophers had fully explained the universe, almost 2,000 years beforehand. So to find something out, instead of conducting an experiment or making a calculation, you read from their writings.

One of the greatest Greeks was Aristotle, who we now know was wrong about almost everything in physics. The powerful Catholic Church of the sixteenth century taught that Aristotle was right, partly because his views fitted with the Bible. So to criticize Aristotle was almost the same as criticizing the Church, which was a very dangerous thing to do. In 1600, Giordano Bruno was burnt at the stake for questioning and criticizing the Church.

One of the things that Aristotle firmly believed was that the Earth was the centre of the universe, and everything revolved around it: the Moon, the planets, the Sun and even the stars. About 450 years after Aristotle's death, in about AD 150, an astronomer called Ptolemy made a map of the universe according to Aristotle's beliefs. Nearly 1,500 years later, when Galileo was born, Ptolemy's map of the universe was still the official one.

A few scientists rejected this idea and believed, correctly, that the Earth and the planets revolved around the Sun. The most famous of these was Nicolaus Copernicus, who wrote a book on the subject twenty years before Galileo's birth.

It would take someone very brave to say publicly that Aristotle and Ptolemy were wrong, someone with a lot of powerful friends, very strong arguments and the skill to make them sound convincing. Someone like Galileo.

IN THEIR OWN WORDS

'There will be many who, when they read my writings, will turn their minds not to reflecting on whether what I have written is true, but solely to seeking how they may, justly or unjustly, undermine my arguments.'

GALILEO, IN ABOUT 1591.

LEFT: *The solar system according to Nicolaus Copernicus, with the Sun at the centre. It was this theory that Galileo argued for, and which led to his conflict with the Church.*

The First Scientist

GALILEO GALILEI (pronounced Ga-li-LAY-oh Ga-li-LAY-ee) was born in the town of Pisa, Italy, on 15 February 1564. His father, Vincenzio, was a musician and amateur scientist who wasn't afraid to challenge the authority of Aristotle. In fact, he enjoyed it. Vincenzio tried to give mathematical explanations of the way music and musical instruments worked, and he got into all sorts of arguments as a result. His son, Galileo, developed his love of mathematics and music from his father, and his argumentative nature, too.

Galileo was the eldest of seven children, and he had four sisters and two brothers. Before the age of ten, he was taught at home by a teacher called Jacopo Borghini. Galileo probably learnt the basics of grammar and mathematics, like many other children of the time. Unlike them, Galileo also liked to build mechanical toys.

BELOW: *Italy in Galileo's time. The inset map shows Italy's position in the world.*

ABOVE: *Galileo was born in this house in Pisa, Italy.*

When Galileo was ten, his family moved to Florence, and Galileo went to school for the first time, at a nearby monastery. He learnt about religion, Latin, mathematics, and what little was known of physics and astronomy. These were all subjects that were going to be very important to him throughout his life. We don't know how Galileo got on at school, but being taught with other students would have given him the chance for plenty of discussions, and probably lots of arguments as well.

At first, Galileo's father wanted him to be a cloth merchant, but Galileo was more interested in science. Vincenzio was happy with this, and decided that Galileo should become a doctor instead. So in 1581, seventeen-year-old Galileo left Florence and returned to Pisa, to study medicine at the university there.

ARGUMENTS

Galileo wasn't very interested in medicine, and he hadn't been at Pisa long before he began to attend maths lectures in his spare time. He got more and more interested in maths, and the lecturer, Ostillo Ricci, encouraged him to study this instead of medicine. When Galileo's father heard about this idea, he didn't like it at all. But in 1584, Galileo went ahead, dropping medicine and beginning a full-time study of mathematics instead.

It wasn't just his father that Galileo argued with. If he disagreed with his fellow students or their lecturers, he would say so, loudly. He was soon known as 'The Wrangler' because of his frequent arguments with just about everyone.

ABOVE: *This fresco, painted in 1841, shows Galileo observing a hanging lamp in the Cathedral of Pisa. It was this observation that led to his discovery of the laws of the pendulum.*

Challenging the ancients

The arguments were usually about the correct way to understand nature. According to scholars at the time, the best approach was to study books by ancient Greek philosophers such as Aristotle, and discuss how they should be interpreted.

IN THEIR OWN WORDS

'I am sure that if Aristotle should return to Earth, he would rather accept me among his followers... than a great many other people who... go pilfering conceptions from his texts that never entered his head.'

GALILEO, IN 1640.

ABOVE: *A modern-day photograph of the Cathedral of Pisa, with the Leaning Tower behind.*

Galileo thought that the explanations should be tested by experiments and observations. Today, all scientists take this for granted, but Galileo was the first person to insist on it. In this way, he was the first true scientist.

The pendulum

Before long, Galileo put his ideas into action. One Sunday, in about 1583, Galileo was attending mass at Pisa Cathedral when he noticed a hanging lamp that had just been lit. It was swinging to and fro, and the lengths of the swings were getting shorter and shorter. Yet Galileo realized that the lamp took the same time to complete a swing, whether the swing was long or short. Galileo did many experiments and eventually found the mathematical law that related the length of a pendulum to the time of its swing.

In 1603, a friend of Galileo's used his discovery to invent a device called a Pulsilogium. This was a pendulum of varying length that could be used to measure people's pulses. It soon became very popular with doctors.

THE PENDULUM

Galileo discovered that a pendulum swings at the same rate, however wide the swings are (within certain limits), and that the rate depends on the length of the string. He also found that the rate of the swing does not depend on the weight of the pendulum.

The motion of a pendulum could not easily be explained by Aristotle's physics, which claimed that a constant push was needed to keep something moving. Galileo's discovery was only fully explained by Albert Einstein, over 300 years later.

Florence and density

After four years at Pisa University, in 1585, 21-year-old Galileo left, without a degree. How was he to earn a living? His father could no longer afford to look after him, and all Galileo had to offer were his scientific skills and plenty of charm. Armed with these, he moved back to Florence, the centre of intellectual and artistic development at the time. He soon managed to find a job there as a mathematics tutor.

In Florence, Galileo studied the work of Archimedes, an ancient Greek mathematician and physicist who lived between 287 and 212 BC. Unlike Aristotle, Archimedes approved of experiments, and he had discovered a way of finding the density of solid materials. In 1586, while working on Archimedes' discovery, Galileo developed an invention called a 'little balance', which was used to take measurements of density.

BELOW: *A painting of the city of Florence in Galileo's time. You can see people fishing in the bottom left of the picture, while an artist sits on a hill in the bottom right. Many artists and writers lived in the city.*

Galileo knew that scientific discoveries were no good unless people understood them, so he wrote *The Little Balance*, which was a book about Archimedes and his new device. He realized that not many people would read a dry, Latin textbook, so he made it entertaining and wrote it in Italian. This book, like his others, not only taught people science, it also showed them how to practise science, using experiment, logic and calculation.

Before long, Galileo made friends with the powerful Marquis Guidobaldo del Monte. In 1589, the marquis found Galileo a job as Professor of Mathematics back in Pisa. The pay was terrible, but Galileo accepted.

ABOVE: *This drawing shows Archimedes experimenting with measuring density using a bath of water. Galileo greatly admired Archimedes and developed an instrument based on his ideas that allowed the accurate determination of density.*

THE GOLDEN CROWN

The weight of a particular volume (such as a cubic centimetre) of a substance is called its density. An ancient legend tells how in 250 BC, Archimedes was asked by King Hieron of Syracuse to find out whether his crown was made of pure gold. Archimedes knew that gold has a particular density. To check the crown's purity, he wanted to compare its density with that of pure gold. If the volume of the crown was the same as the volume of a piece of gold of the same weight, that would prove their densities were the same and that the crown was pure.

Archimedes was sitting in the bath one day when he realized how to measure the crown's volume: if he had a bath full of water and sank the crown in it, the volume of the water that overflowed would be the volume of the crown. In this way, Archimedes discovered that the crown was not pure gold.

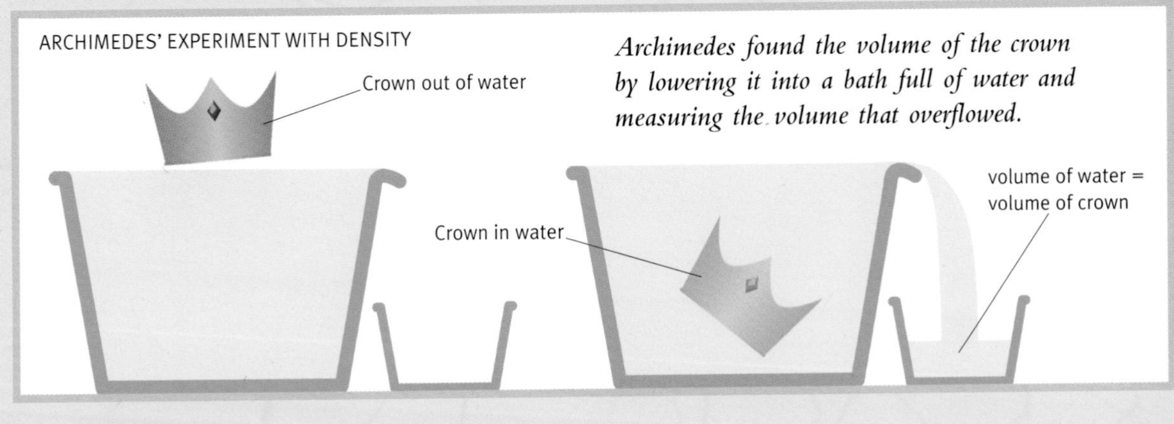

Archimedes found the volume of the crown by lowering it into a bath full of water and measuring the volume that overflowed.

Laws of Movement

BACK IN PISA, 23-year-old Galileo tried to convince people that Aristotle's approach was wrong. He was soon involved in bitter arguments. Though he could be very charming, Galileo could also be insulting, and he started to make enemies.

Meanwhile, Galileo was trying to work out the laws that describe the movement of objects. He tried to use observation, experiment, logic and calculation, which was the method he knew was correct. We would now call this method 'the scientific method'. Galileo described his work in a book called *On Motion*, but when it was finished, he realized that he had made all sorts of statements with no proper evidence to back them up, just like Aristotle himself. So Galileo cancelled the book's publication.

BELOW: *This fresco shows Galileo demonstrating the law of gravity in Pisa. You can see the cathedral and the Leaning Tower in the background.*

GRAVITY, ACCELERATION AND AIR RESISTANCE

Galileo discovered that the speed of falling objects does not depend on their weights. He also found that their speeds increase: in other words, they accelerate. Isaac Newton later showed that the reason for this acceleration is the constant gravitational pull of the Earth.

Sometimes, light things do fall more slowly than heavy ones: for example, feathers fall slower than stones. But that is because of the resistance of the air. In a vacuum, feathers, stones and other objects fall at the same speed. The spheres in Galileo's demonstration did not hit the ground exactly together because of air resistance.

BELOW: *The Leaning Tower of Pisa is a bell tower that was built between 1173 and 1370. It leans 4.4 metres out of line from its seventh storey because it was built on unstable soil. Today, engineers are trying to strengthen the tower's foundations and straighten it a little, to stop it falling over.*

Challenging Aristotle

Aristotle had said that it was a law of nature that heavier objects fell faster than light ones. Galileo was sure this wasn't true. He had noticed that in a hailstorm, heavy and light hailstones fell together, and he'd done experiments to test his idea. But knowing that he was right wasn't enough. Galileo knew that he had to convince others, too. He did this in a very public way, by dropping objects from the top of the Leaning Tower of Pisa in 1591, watched by a crowd of people from the university (see pages 4–5).

Although proving he was correct must have been a great moment for Galileo, he soon received some devastating news: his father had died. Not only that, he was now responsible by law for his father's expenses, including a dowry for his sister, Virginia. And, as if things weren't bad enough, his three-year contract at the university came to an end. Galileo had upset too many people for it to be renewed. He was out of a job.

Padua and Pinelli

IT WAS JUST as well that Galileo had made friends as well as enemies. Guidobaldo del Monte, who had found Galileo his last job, soon found him another maths professorship. But this one, at Padua University, had a good salary. In 1592, at the age of twenty-eight, Galileo moved to Padua and stayed in the house of another powerful friend, Gianvincenzo Pinelli.

Pinelli's house had two big advantages: it had an amazing library, which Galileo was allowed to use, and it was visited by some of the most powerful people in the city. So Galileo now had money, access to a world of knowledge and the chance to make more influential friends.

RIGHT: *Guidobaldo del Monte was Galileo's friend as well as a patron.*

Galileo did not stay as Pinelli's guest for very long. He soon moved to a house of his own, with enough space for a workshop. There he built scientific instruments, both to use himself and to sell.

However, Galileo had bad times in Padua, too. He enjoyed drinking almost as much as arguing about science. One night, after an evening of drinking with three friends, he fell asleep with them in a room that had an opening in the wall. The opening led to a cold, damp cave. Both of his friends became ill and died. Galileo caught a severe chill and was troubled with rheumatism for the rest of his life.

IN THEIR OWN WORDS

'Philosophy is written in this grand book... the universe... which stands continually open to our gaze, but it cannot be understood unless one first learns to comprehend the language in which it is written. It is written in the language of mathematics.'

GALILEO, FROM HIS BOOK *THE ASSAYER*, IN 1623.

BELOW: *An engraving made in 1630 showing the University of Padua, where Galileo was Professor of Mathematics from 1592 until 1610.*

How Does the World Work?

NOW THAT HE had solved the mystery of falling objects, Galileo was investigating a more difficult question. What happened if objects weren't dropped, but thrown? How would they move? This was an important question, which could be applied to the motion of projectiles, such as cannonballs and arrows.

ABOVE: *Cannon being used to lay siege to a city in 1570. Galileo knew there was money to be made if he improved the way cannons were used.*

BALLISTICS

According to Aristotle, an object could only move in one direction at once. So he believed that when a cannonball was fired from a cannon, it moved in straight lines. At first, the force of the cannon made the cannonball go in a straight, diagonal line, up through the air. When this force was used up, the cannonball would fall straight down to the ground.

Galileo soon realized that this was completely wrong, and that cannonballs moved in smooth curves. His studies allowed him to show that to travel as far as possible, a cannon must be aimed at an angle of 45 degrees to the ground.

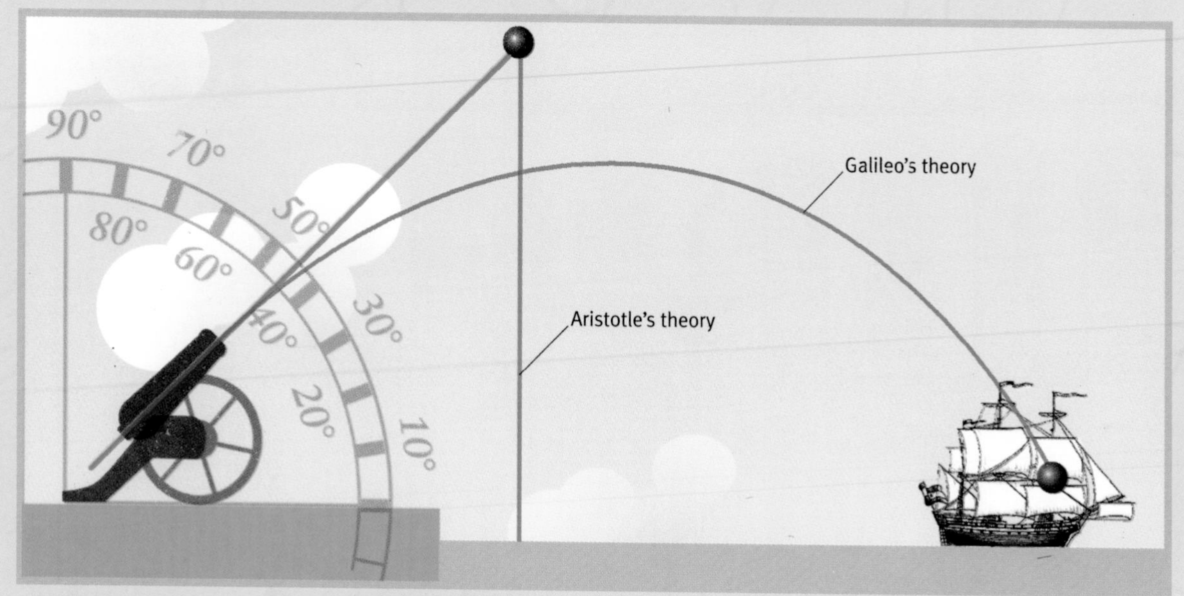

The military compass

The army in Italy was powerful, rich and interested in any scientific developments to do with weapons. Being a great practical scientist, in 1597, Galileo developed a tool that could be used to aim cannons. It could also calculate the amount of gunpowder needed for different sizes and types of cannonball, and perform many other forms of calculation and measurement. Galileo called his invention a 'military compass', which was a clever way to interest the army. The military compass was the direct ancestor of the pocket calculator. Soon it was so popular that Galileo had to employ an assistant to supply all the orders he received for it.

BELOW: *Johannes Kepler, an enthusiastic supporter of Galileo's theories, who discovered the mathematical laws of planetary motion. He also proved that the planets move around the Sun in ellipses, not circles as Galileo believed.*

Astronomy

In 1597, Galileo, now aged thirty-three, became increasingly interested in astronomy. Jacopo Mannoni, a fellow mathematician who Galileo used to work with, argued that the appearance of the sky throughout the year proved that the Earth did not move. Galileo was almost sure that it did, and he was able to show that Mannoni was wrong. In the same year, Johannes Kepler, a German astronomer and mathematician, published a book arguing that the Earth moved round the Sun. He wrote to Galileo, asking for his support. Though Galileo agreed with him, he knew it would be too dangerous to say so publicly.

MAGNETISM AND MEASUREMENT

In about 1599, while still living in Padua, 35-year-old Galileo met a woman called Maria Gamba. She became his mistress for many years and in 1600 and 1601, she gave birth to his two daughters, Virginia and Livia. To begin with, the two girls lived with their grandmother, Galileo's mother. But they were unhappy there, so when they each reached the age of sixteen, Galileo moved them to a convent not far from where he lived. He and Virginia were very fond of each other and exchanged many letters over the years. Over a hundred of Virginia's letters still survive. They give an interesting insight into the time. The girls' mother, Maria, married someone else.

BELOW: *This engraving made in Galileo's time shows a scientist investigating magnetism in his laboratory. At the bottom-left of the engraving, a lodestone (natural magnet) rests on a floating board in a bowl of water. It would turn itself so that the same part always pointed North, like the needles of the compasses on the two tables.*

Magnetism

One of Galileo's scientific interests at this time was magnetism. In 1600, the English physician William Gilbert discovered that the Earth was a gigantic magnet. Magnets became the latest craze and all the rich people wanted one. Galileo, as practical as ever, developed ways of making magnets more powerful. But he was not content with Gilbert's approach of explaining the way magnets worked in words. He knew that the most accurate description would be a mathematical one.

Law of falling objects

In 1608, Galileo was still investigating the law of falling objects, but objects that fell through space moved too quickly for their changes in speed to be measured. So Galileo developed a clever method of rolling balls down sloping boards instead. There was no instrument available for him to measure times accurately in seconds. Instead, he may have placed threads across the boards at regular intervals, and used the clicks made by the balls as they rolled over the threads to find out how their speed changed. He also used a simple water clock.

Galileo found that falling objects accelerate according to a simple rule (see box). He was trying to prove exactly why this was when his work was interrupted and his attention drawn to the sky by something amazing: a new star.

ABOVE: *William Gilbert demonstrating the power of static electricity to Queen Elizabeth I of England. When an amber rod is rubbed, it becomes charged and will attract light objects like feathers. Gilbert made many discoveries about magnetism, and realised that the Earth is a giant magnet.*

GALILEO'S LAW OF FALL

Galileo found that however fast an object is falling after a certain time, after twice the time it will be falling twice as fast, and after three times the time it will be falling three times as fast, and so on.

The Changing Sky

IN 1604, a bright new star appeared in the sky. According to Aristotle, the stars and planets were made of a mysterious substance, called 'the fifth essence', which was not found on Earth. Stars and planets were supposed to be perfect spheres, moving in perfect circles for ever, with no change of any kind. Yet the new star seemed to show they *could* change.

BELOW: *This image was made by a computer to show how a star explodes as a supernova.*

SUPERNOVAE

We now know that what Galileo saw in 1604 wasn't really the beginning of a new star. It was the end of an old one. Supernovae are enormous explosions, which sometimes take place when stars die. The explosion seen in 1604 happened because there was a pair of stars close together in space. Over a long period, material from one star fell on to the other. Eventually, the mass of the second star became so great that the matter inside it was hot and crushed enough to set up runaway nuclear reactions. These led to a gigantic explosion, in which the pair of stars became about 100 million times brighter than the Sun.

All over Europe, arguments raged about what the new star meant. Galileo was soon involved in a public dispute with Cesare Cremonini. He was a friend and fellow mathematician, but also a devoted follower of Aristotle. Cremonini thought that, to explain the star's appearance, it had to be in the Earth's atmosphere. But Galileo knew that if that was true, the new star's position in the sky compared to the other stars would change, depending on where it was seen from, which it didn't. So he concluded, along with Johannes Kepler, that the star was outside the Earth's atmosphere, far beyond the Moon's orbit.

Two years later, in 1606, Galileo's son was born. He was named Vincenzio, after Galileo's father.

By 1609, Galileo was becoming well known, and he was sometimes asked to write horoscopes for people. We don't know how seriously Galileo took the horoscopes, but they certainly didn't work. In 1609, he predicted a long and happy life for Ferdinand I de Medici, the Grand Duke of Tuscany. Ferdinand died twenty-two days later.

RIGHT: *In about 1606, Galileo built a primitive type of thermometer called a thermoscope. To prepare it, the sphere was heated. Then the tube was placed in liquid (usually water or wine). As the air in the sphere cooled, it contracted, taking up less space, so the liquid was drawn partly up the tube. Changes in temperature were shown by the height of the liquid in the tube. The cooler the sphere, the higher the liquid reached.*

THE TELESCOPE

In about 1608, the telescope was invented, probably in Holland, by an optician called Hans Lippershey (1570–1619). The telescope was to lead to the best and worst experiences of Galileo's life.

A year later, working from no more than a vague description, Galileo built his own, much better telescope. Telescopes rapidly became famous, and in 1609, Galileo presented his version to the Doge (chief magistrate) of Venice. It could magnify objects nine times. The Doge was so impressed that he promised Galileo a permanent, well-paid job in exchange for his telescope. The job sounded wonderful, and Galileo accepted. But when he got to Venice, Galileo found that the job was nothing like the one he'd been promised, and he angrily returned to Florence.

BELOW: *A fresco showing Galileo demonstrating his telescope to the Doge of Venice in 1609.*

TELESCOPES

The first telescopes were very basic. The images they showed were blurred and full of coloured bands. They were also upside-down. Galileo's telescopes, made with more carefully shaped lenses and equipped with special fittings, gave much sharper images, which were the right way up.

Galileo made the best telescopes there were and he sold many of them. His first telescope enlarged things three times, but he soon made one that magnified objects more than thirty times.

ABOVE: *A modern reconstruction of one of Galileo's telescopes, in Florence.*

Galileo soon found another wealthy person who loved the telescope: the Grand Duke Cosimo. After some dramatic demonstrations of the telescope's power, Cosimo offered Galileo a job, back in Florence. This time, the job was as good as it sounded.

But this turned out to be a bad move for Galileo. By moving to Florence, which was under the control of the Catholic Church in Rome, Galileo would have to be much more careful not to offend the Church. Unfortunately he was about to do just that.

The New Solar System

THE TELESCOPE was more than just a way of getting jobs for Galileo. Since before 4000 BC, people had been interested in the stars and had made careful observations and measurements of them. But in all those thousands of years they had been limited by the power of their eyesight. It was assumed that there was no more to the sky than could be seen with the naked eye.

In 1609, Galileo pointed a telescope at the night sky that could enlarge objects over thirty times. He discovered a whole new universe. Within seconds, Galileo discovered stars that had never been seen before. Within days he'd made amazing discoveries which completely demolished Aristotle's ideas of a solar system made up of perfectly smooth planets, all moving in perfect circles around the Earth.

Galileo saw that there were mountains on the Moon just as on the Earth, and that the planet Jupiter was surrounded by four companions. After a few nights, Galileo was sure that these companions were new moons orbiting Jupiter. Yet Aristotle had insisted that everything in space must orbit the Earth.

ABOVE: *A modern photograph of the surface of the Moon, using a powerful telescope.*

IN THEIR OWN WORDS

'It is a most beautiful and delightful sight to behold the body of the moon... it certainly does not possess a smooth and polished surface, but one rough and uneven, and just like the face of the Earth itself, it is everywhere full of vast protuberances, deep chasms, and sinuosities...'

GALILEO, FROM *THE STARRY MESSENGER*, 1610.

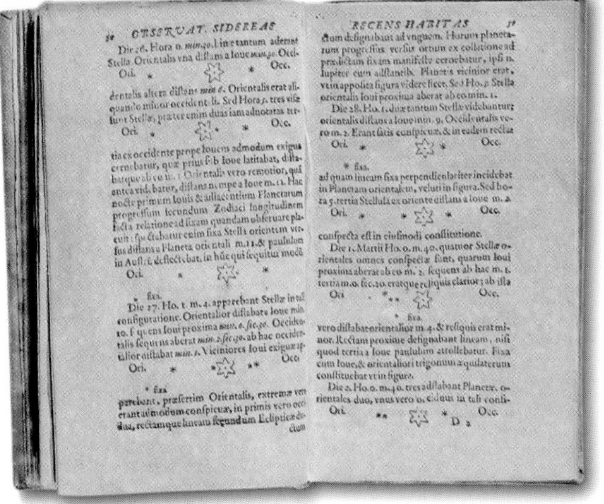

30 OBSERVAT. SIDEREAS

Die 26. Hora 0. *min.30.* Binæ tantum aderant Stellæ. Orientalis vna distans a Ioue *min.30.* Occi-

Ori. * ✡ * Occ.

dentalis altera distans *min.6.* Orientalis erat aliquando minor occidentali. Sed Hora 5. tres visæ sunt Stellæ, præter enim duas iam adnotatas ter-

Ori. * ✡ * * Occ.

tia ex occidente prope Iouem admodum exigua cernebatur, quæ prius sub Ioue latitabat, [illegible] Orientalis vero remotior, quã antea videbatur, distans nempe a Ioue m. 11. Hac nocte primum Iouis & adiacentium Planetarum progressum secundum Zodiaci longitudinem facta relatione ad fixam quandam obseruare placuit: spectabatur enim fixa Stella orientem versus distans a Planeta orientali m. 11. & paululum in Austrũ deflectebat, in hũc qui sequitur modũ

Ori. * ✡ *

* fixa

Die 27. Ho. 1. m. 4. apparebant Stellæ in tali configuratione. Orientalior distabat a Ioue min. 10. sequens Ioui proxima *min. 0. sec. 30.* Occidentalis sequens aberat *min. 2. sec. 30.* ab hac occidentalior distabat *min. 1.* Viciniores Ioui exiguæ apparebant, præsertim Orientalis, extremæ vero erant admodum conspicuæ, in primis vero occidua, rectamque lineam secundum Eclipticæ ductum

RECENS HABITAS 31

ctum designabant ad vnguem. Horum planetarum progressus versus ortum ex collatione ad prædictam fixam manifeste cernebatur, ipsi n. Iupiter cum adstantib. Planetis vicinior erat, vt in apposita figura videre licet. Sed Ho. 5. Stella orientalis Ioui proxima aberat ab eo min. 1.

Die 28. Ho. 1. duæ tantum Stellæ videbantur; orientalis distans a Ioue min. 9. Occidentalis vero m. 2. Erant satis conspicuæ, & in eadem recta

Ori. * ✡ * Occ.

* fixa.

ad quam lineam fixa perpendiculariter incidebat in Planetam orientalem, veluti in figura. Sed hora 5. tertia Stellula ex oriente distans a Ioue m. 2

Ori. * * ✡ * Occ.

conspecta est in eiusmodi constitutione.

Die 1. Martii Ho. 0. m. 40. quatuor Stellæ orientales omnes conspectæ sunt, quarum Ioui proxima aberat ab eo m. 2. sequens ab hac m. 1. tertia m. 0. sec. 20. eratque reliquis clarior; ab illa

Ori. * * * ✡ Occ.

* fixa.

vero distabat orientalior m. 4. & reliquis erat minor. Rectam proxime designabant lineam, nisi quod tertia a Ioue paululum attollebatur. Fixa cum Ioue, & orientaliori trigonum æquilaterum constituebat vt in figura.

Die 2. Ho. 0. m. 40. tres adstabant Planetæ, orientales duo, vnus vero occiduus in tali confi-

Ori. * * ✡ * Occ.

D 2

ABOVE: *Part of Galileo's book* The Starry Messenger, *with his drawings of Jupiter and its moons. From the way their positions changed from night to night, he was able to work out how long it took each moon to orbit Jupiter.*

In 1610, when Galileo moved to Florence to start his new job, he made yet more discoveries. He found that the planet Venus was sometimes seen as a large crescent, and at other times as a small disc. This only made sense if Venus orbited the Sun. And when Galileo turned his telescope to Saturn, the most distant planet known, he found that it changed shape in a mysterious way. It was not until better telescopes were developed that it was discovered that Saturn's odd appearance was due to the rings around it. That year, in 1610, Galileo published his amazing discoveries in a book called *The Starry Messenger*, which immediately became a bestseller.

BELOW: *Jupiter and the moons that Galileo discovered: Ganymede, Europa, Io and Callisto. They are now called the Galilean moons. This image was created by putting together individual photographs of the moons, taken from the* Voyager *spacecraft in 1979.*

ABOVE: *Galileo in St Mark's Square in Venice, using a telescope he had built to show the moons of Jupiter to city officials.*

IN THEIR OWN WORDS

'What would you say of the learned [educated] here, who, replete with [full of] the pertinacity of the asp [stubbornness of the snake] have steadfastly refused to cast a glance through the telescope? Shall we laugh or shall we cry?'

GALILEO, IN A LETTER TO JOHANNES KEPLER, IN ABOUT 1610.

FAME AND MISFORTUNE

In 1611, Galileo visited Rome, where he demonstrated the power of his telescope to various rich citizens in the city. Together with his book, *The Starry Messenger*, these demonstrations made Galileo famous throughout Italy. He was soon invited to join The Lincean Academy (which means 'academy of the lynx-eyed'), the world's first scientific society.

Galileo was soon involved in another public debate. A German astronomer called Christoph Scheiner (1573-1650) had been using telescopes to observe the Sun when he noticed dark spots. Like all followers of Aristotle, Scheiner believed that the Sun

SUNSPOTS

By observing the changing appearances of sunspots, Galileo concluded that they had to be markings on the Sun itself. Their shapes changed just like blotches on a rotating sphere. By studying the speeds of the changing shapes, Galileo also found out that the Sun must rotate on its axis about once a month. What he didn't know was what the sunspots were actually made of. We now know that sunspots are cooler parts of the Sun's surface, caused by intense magnetic fields.

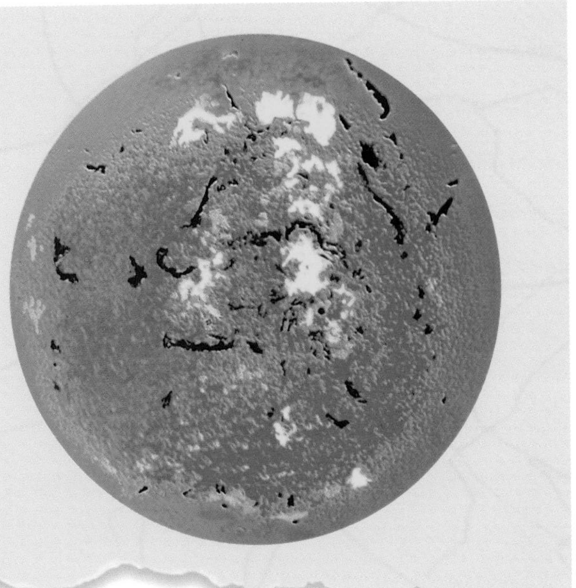

ABOVE: *A specially coloured photograph showing the different features of the Sun's surface. Sunspots are coloured yellow.*

itself was perfect and unmarked, which meant that the spots had to be caused by something between the Sun and the Earth. Scheiner wrote a book putting forward his conclusions.

Galileo completely disagreed with Scheiner. It was obvious to him that the spots were on the Sun's surface. He published a series of letters, criticizing Scheiner's idea and also clearly stating his belief that the Earth moved around the Sun. This was a dangerous move. By challenging Scheiner, Galileo was challenging Aristotle and the teachings of the Church. Things got even more serious when Thomas Caccini, a Catholic friar, preached a sermon condemning science in general, and Galileo in particular.

Meanwhile, many Catholics were trying to prove that Galileo was wrong. Some were so sure that he was, they refused even to look through telescopes to check! One Catholic argued that the moons of Jupiter could not exist because they were of no use to people, so God wouldn't have created them.

IN THEIR OWN WORDS

'...certain discoveries that depart from common and popular opinions have been noisily denied... obliging me to hide in silence every new idea of mine until I have more than proved it.'

GALILEO TO MARK WELSER, A BANKER AND ARCHAEOLOGIST, IN ABOUT 1610.

IN THEIR OWN WORDS

'...the said Galileo was by the said Commissary commanded and enjoined, in the name of his Holiness the Pope and the whole Congregation of the Holy Office, to relinquish altogether the said opinion that the Sun is the centre of the world and immovable and that the Earth moves; nor further to hold, teach or defend it in any way whatsoever, verbally or in writing...'

FROM THE INACCURATE REPORT OF GALILEO'S MEETING WITH CARDINAL BELLARMINE.

TROUBLE WITH THE CHURCH

Galileo's enemies, having failed to outwit him in scientific debates, now attacked him on religious grounds. This was much more dangerous for Galileo. Even though he was religious, he was quite sure that the Bible was wrong when it came to scientific matters, but he didn't dare say so. After Caccini's sermon in 1614 (see page 29), the idea that the Earth might go round the Sun amounted to an attack on the Bible, and Galileo's *Sunspot Letters* clearly supported the idea.

Galileo decided to deal with this question at the highest level, so in 1615, he set out to Rome to discuss it with the Pope. This was a mistake. Pope Paul V was not impressed by scientific arguments, and set up a commission to decide whether Galileo's views were acceptable or not. The commission did not consider whether Galileo's ideas were supported by scientific evidence. They only asked whether they contradicted the Bible. The commission soon decided that they did, and that to believe that the Earth moved around the Sun amounted to criticizing the Bible.

LEFT: *Pope Paul V, leader of the Catholic Church from 1605 to 1621.*

Galileo was not punished, but he was told off by the Pope's assistant, Cardinal Bellarmine, and forbidden to state that the Earth moved.

Although Galileo had got off lightly, the seeds had been sown for more trouble later. The Pope had said that if Galileo resisted the commission's instruction and insisted that the Earth moved, he would be forbidden even to discuss the idea of a moving Earth ever again. Galileo did not resist, so he was not forbidden to discuss the idea again. But his enemies wrote a report saying that he had been forbidden. Galileo knew nothing of this, so he didn't realize the danger of discussing his ideas. However, he cleverly managed to get an accurate report signed by Bellarmine, in case he ever needed it. Seventeen years later, he did.

BELOW: *The Pope and his cardinals in Rome were very powerful in Galileo's time. This painting shows cardinals and other members of the Vatican with Galileo, at his later visit in 1633.*

A Dangerous Debate

After his 1615 meeting with the Pope, it would have been safer for Galileo to avoid discussing astronomy. But keeping quiet wasn't in his nature, especially when in 1618, something happened in the sky that no one could ignore, even people who refused to look through telescopes. One after another, three bright comets appeared.

We now know that comets are normally millions of kilometres from Earth but, according to Aristotle, they had to exist in the Earth's atmosphere because he believed that nothing beyond the Moon ever changed. In 1619, a religious astronomer called Orazio Grassi wrote a book claiming that comets circled the Earth. The same year, Galileo launched an attack on Grassi and his theory in a book called *Discourse on the Comets*. In reply, Grassi and his colleagues wrote *The Astronomical and Philosophical Balance*, which criticized Galileo's views for being unscientific and irreligious. In 1623, Galileo wrote yet another book in reply: *The Assayer*. Again, he argued for the idea of a moving Earth.

BELOW: *The Hale-Bopp comet travelled to less than 197 million kilometres from the Earth's surface in March 1997. Its nucleus, or centre, was about 35 kilometres wide. At night, this bright comet was easily visible with the naked eye.*

COMETS

Comets originate in a cloud of icy objects beyond Pluto, the outermost planet. From time to time, they leave this cloud and move through the solar system, attracted by the gravitational pull of the Sun. When they approach the Sun, the ice starts to evaporate, and jets of dust and gas form long tails, which stretch away from the comet through space. It is at this stage that comets are sometimes visible from Earth.

LEFT: *The title page of* The Assayer, *in which Galileo argued for a new approach to science. The cherubs at the top of the page are holding the military compass that Galileo invented (left) and a telescope (right).*

IN THEIR OWN WORDS

'He tells me that with this long tube, he has seen flies which look as big as a lamb, and has learned that they are all covered in hair.'

GIOVANNI DU PONT, WRITING ABOUT GALILEO'S MICROSCOPE IN 1614.

BELOW: *Pope Urban VIII.*

Galileo probably didn't think that claiming the Earth moved was too dangerous, because by now there was a new Pope in Rome, Urban VIII. Not only was Urban interested in science, he had also been a good friend to Galileo. At first it seemed that Galileo was safe. The Pope even had *The Assayer* read to him at his meals because it was so entertaining!

In 1624, the Pope invited Galileo to visit him in Rome. Unlike his previous visit, there was no criticism of his support for the idea of a moving Earth. In fact, Galileo hoped to convince his old friend that the Earth really moved. He soon found this was impossible, but the two got on very well and the Pope was delighted with a microscope that Galileo made for him.

Which Universe?

While Galileo was sure that the Earth and other planets moved around the Sun, the Pope still insisted that the Sun and planets moved around the Earth. But he agreed that Galileo should write a book, presenting the arguments for and against these two theories of the universe. However, Galileo was not allowed to come to the conclusion that the Earth moved. He was only allowed to present it as a possibility.

Galileo was very pleased to have the chance to discuss the theory of a moving Earth, and started to write the book, called *Dialogue Concerning the Two Chief Systems of the World*. It took him eight years to complete the book and as usual, Galileo made it as entertaining and readable as possible. He presented it in the form of a conversation between three people: one agreed with Copernicus that the Earth moved, one agreed with Aristotle that it didn't and one was supposed to be neutral.

IN THEIR OWN WORDS

'The Bible shows the way to go to Heaven, not the way the heavens go.'

GALILEO.

LEFT: *The title page of* Dialogue Concerning the Two Chief Systems of the World, *the book which revolutionized science – and led to Galileo's downfall.*

As well as discussing the idea that the Earth moved, the book contained many other important ideas, including the beginnings of the theory of relativity. Galileo pointed out that objects in the hold of a ship behave in the same way whether the ship is motionless or moving smoothly. This seems obvious now, but it was a new way of looking at the world, and over the next three centuries, scientists were to develop this idea into a theory that explained the whole universe.

When the book was finished at last, in 1632, it showed all Galileo's skill as a scientist and writer. But he had found it impossible to keep the two arguments in balance. It was clear to everyone who read it that it supported the theory of a moving Earth. The book was one of the most important ever written, but for Galileo it was a disaster.

ABOVE: *The Sun and planets of the solar system (not to scale): from the top left, they are Mercury, Venus, Earth and its moon, Mars, Jupiter, Saturn, Uranus, Neptune and Pluto and its moon Charon. The three outer planets were unknown in Galileo's time.*

Crime and Punishment

THE POPE HATED Galileo's book. For one thing, Galileo's enemies had told him that one of the characters in the book was based on Urban himself, and this character was portrayed as slow-witted. This was untrue, but it was obvious that Galileo had not stuck to his agreement to write a balanced book. He had not been able to resist showing that Copernicus was right: the Earth did move. Galileo had made many enemies with his earlier writings, and they did all they could to stir up the Pope's anger against him.

Once again, the matter was referred to a committee, which decided that Galileo had not done as he had agreed, and that the book should be banned. In 1632, Galileo was summoned to Rome to explain himself.

By this time, Galileo was sixty-eight and suffering from rheumatism, so he asked to be allowed to stay where he was. But even when three doctors signed a letter stating that Galileo was seriously unwell, the Pope replied by saying that if Galileo did not obey him, he would send men to bring him to Rome in chains. And if Galileo was too ill to be moved, the men would wait until he was recovered enough for the journey.

RIGHT: *Galileo and Urban VIII, meeting in 1633.*

So Galileo made the long trip to Rome again and was put on trial. The Pope had the power to put him to death, torture him, or lock him up for the rest of his life. If Galileo hadn't been clever enough to have a signed record made of his earlier visit to Rome, any of these things might have happened. When the false record was read out, claiming that Galileo had been forbidden to discuss the idea of a moving Earth, he responded by reading the accurate one. But Galileo could not hope to win. He was forced to make a statement saying that the Earth did not move, was forbidden to write anything further and was sentenced to imprisonment for life.

IN THEIR OWN WORDS

'Who can doubt that it will lead to the worst disorders when minds created free by God are compelled to submit slavishly to an outside will? When we are told to deny our senses and subject them to the whim of others? When people of whatsoever competence are made judges over experts and are granted authority to treat them as they please?'

GALILEO, AFTER HIS SENTENCE IN 1633.

BELOW: *Galileo's trial in the Vatican, in 1633.*

ABOVE: *In his old age, Galileo was visited by many people, including the poet John Milton.*

THE END OF SCIENCE?

Luckily, Galileo had many friends as well as enemies, and they spoke to the Pope. Before long, his sentence was softened slightly and he was allowed to serve his life-long imprisonment in his own home. So in 1633, at the age of sixty-nine, Galileo returned to Florence for the last time. The long journeys and the terrors of his trial had left him seriously ill, and he was made even more miserable when his beloved daughter, Virginia, died soon after, on 2 April, 1634.

For some time, Galileo was so sickened by what had happened that he turned his back on science, returning to his earlier interests in music and painting. But before long, 70-year-old Galileo was at work again. One of the friends who had helped him during the trial was Archbishop Piccolomini, and they worked together on science in Galileo's house, although they avoided the question of the Earth's motion.

Despite the Pope's ban on writing anything new, Galileo was soon hard at work writing a book called *Discourse Concerning Two New Sciences*. One of these new sciences was that of moving objects, and Galileo explained clearly how things move when they are dropped or thrown, or when they roll down slopes or swing from side to side. The other new science mainly concerned the strength of materials, in particular the effect of the size of an object on its strength. Galileo also discussed the possible existence of atoms, the weight of the air, the speed of light and of sound and, like his father, the scientific nature of musical sounds. Although his answers weren't all correct, Galileo's book was the beginning of the subjects now called dynamics and engineering science.

IN THEIR OWN WORDS

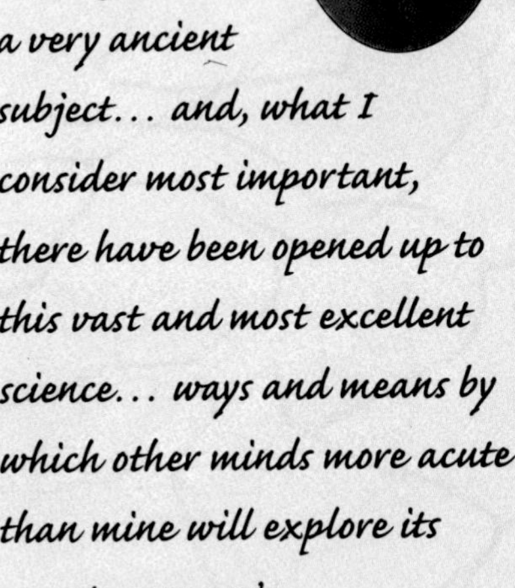

'My purpose is to set forth a very new science dealing with a very ancient subject... and, what I consider most important, there have been opened up to this vast and most excellent science... ways and means by which other minds more acute than mine will explore its remote corners.'

GALILEO, FROM *DISCOURSE CONCERNING TWO NEW SCIENCES*, 1638.

LEFT: *Galileo, blind and near the end of his life, but still working with his pupils and assistants Evangelista Torricelli and Vincenzio Viviani.*

NEW SCIENCE

Although Galileo remained a prisoner for the last eight years of his life, he was not entirely cut off from the outside world. He was famous throughout Europe and was visited by many people, including the poet John Milton and the philosopher Thomas Hobbes. His son, Vincenzio, helped him with some of his work, and he took on two scientific assistants, Vincenzio Viviani and Evangelista Torricelli. He also managed to publish *Two New Sciences*, in 1638, although the manuscript had to be smuggled to Holland to do so.

BELOW: *Galileo, now blind, dictating the principles of a time mechanism to his son Vincenzio.*

In 1637, Galileo went blind, but even this did not stop him from working. He went back to his very first scientific discovery, the pendulum, and used it to solve the problem of how to measure time accurately.

Primitive mechanical clocks had been invented about four centuries earlier, but they were very inaccurate, sometimes losing or gaining more than 15 minutes in a single day. Although Galileo had discovered that a pendulum swings with a regular beat more than half a century earlier, no one had linked a pendulum to a clock mechanism. In 1637, Galileo explained to his son how this could be done. Vincenzio planned and started to build a machine that would have been the heart of the first accurate clock.

In January 1642, at the age of seventy-seven, Galileo Galilei died in the villa in Arcetri, near Florence, which had been his prison for the last eight years.

BELOW: *A model of the time mechanism Galileo invented. His son drew a detailed diagram from Galileo's description. This model was made from the diagram in the nineteenth century.*

IN THEIR OWN WORDS

'Today news has come of the loss of Signor Galilei, which touches not just Florence but the whole world, and our whole century which from this divine man has received more splendour than from almost all the other ordinary philosophers. Now... the sublimity of that intellect will... serve all posterity as a guide in the search for truth.'

REPORT OF GALILEO'S DEATH BY LUKE HOLSTE, LIBRARIAN TO CARDINAL BARBERINI IN ROME, IN A LETTER TO GIOVANNI BATTISTA ON 18 JANUARY, 1642.

The Legacy of Galileo

GALILEO'S SON, Vincenzio, died before he could complete the pendulum clock Galileo had devised. But in 1657, a Dutch scientist called Christiaan Huygens had the same idea and used it to build clocks. Soon, pendulum clocks started to appear all over the world, bringing in a new era of accuracy.

In 1642, the year Galileo died, Isaac Newton was born. Newton soon joined the growing number of scientists who continued Galileo's work. Newton used both Galileo's discoveries and his mathematical approach to develop an enormously successful theory, capable of explaining and predicting the way objects move both on the Earth and beyond it. Combined with his theory of gravitation, Newton was able to calculate exactly how the planets move around the Sun. More than 250 years after Galileo's death, Albert Einstein developed a complete theory of the universe based on the principle of relativity that Galileo had been the first to state.

RIGHT: *The Hubble Space Telescope about to be released from the space-shuttle that transported it into orbit, high above the Earth's surface.*

LEFT: *In 1995, a space probe named after Galileo reached the planet Jupiter. This image shows a model of the Galileo probe.*

Since Galileo's death, telescopes have been developed that are thousands of times more powerful than his, although the biggest are now based on Newton's design, using a mirror instead of a lens. Telescopes have allowed scientists to continue Galileo's exploration of the universe, with amazing results. Dozens of new moons have been added to the four that Galileo discovered, three new planets have been found in our solar system and many more have been found in orbit around distant stars.

Probes have now visited all the planets and moons that Galileo could see. Astronauts have walked on the rugged lunar surface that Galileo discovered, and both astronauts and probes reached their destinations using the laws of motion that Galileo began to formulate.

As far as the Church is concerned, progress was slower. It was 193 years after Galileo's death before the Church lifted the ban on his book, *Dialogue Concerning the Two Chief Systems of the World*, and not until 1965 did a pope speak favourably of Galileo. Finally, 350 years after Galileo's death, his theories were publicly accepted by Pope John Paul II, in 1992. There was no apology.

IN THEIR OWN WORDS

'The discovery and use of scientific reasoning by Galileo was one of the most important achievements in the history of human thought, and marks the real beginning of physics. This discovery taught us that intuitive conclusions based on immediate observation are not always to be trusted, for they sometimes lead to the wrong clues.'

ALBERT EINSTEIN, IN 1938.

Timeline

About 350 BC

Aristotle states that the Sun and the planets revolve around the Earth.

About AD 150

Ptolemy produces his detailed theory of an Earth-centred universe.

1543

Nicolaus Copernicus publishes *On the Revolutions of the Celestial Spheres*, putting forward the idea that the Earth and planets revolve around the Sun.

1564

15 February: Galileo is born in Pisa, Italy.

1574

Galileo's family moves to Florence, Italy.

1581-5

Galileo studies medicine, and then mathematics, at Pisa University.

About 1583

Galileo discovers the pendulum law.

1586

Galileo constructs the hydrostatic balance and writes *The Little Balance*.

1589

Galileo becomes a professor of mathematics at Pisa University.

1591

Galileo demonstrates the law of falling objects from the Leaning Tower of Pisa.
His father dies.

1592

Galileo becomes a professor of mathematics at the University of Padua.

1597

Galileo invents the military compass.
Johannes Kepler discovers that planets revolve around the Sun.

1599

Galileo meets Maria Gamba.

1600

Galileo's daughter, Virginia, is born.
William Gilbert (1544-1603) discovers that the Earth is a gigantic magnet.

1601

Galileo's daughter, Livia, is born.

1604

A supernova appears.

About 1605

Johannes Kepler calculates the elliptical shape of the orbit of Mars.

1606

Galileo's son, Vincenzio, is born.

1608

Hans Lippershey (1570-1619) invents the telescope.

1609

Galileo hears about the telescope and makes an improved version. He observes mountains on the Moon and the moons of Jupiter.
Johannes Kepler publishes his conclusion that the planets move in ellipses.

1610

Galileo moves to Florence, where he observes the changing shapes of Venus and Saturn. Publishes *The Starry Messenger*.

1611

Galileo visits Rome and demonstrates the power of his telescope.
Elected to the Lincean Academy.

1612

Christoph Scheiner writes a book on sunspots.

1613

Galileo publishes his theory of sunspots, including a clear statement that the Earth orbits the Sun.

1614

Thomas Caccini preaches against science, and Galileo.

1615

Galileo goes to Rome to discuss his theories of the universe with Pope Paul V. The Pope refers the question to a committee.

1616

Galileo is told not to state that the Earth moves.

1618

Three comets appear.

1619

Galileo disagrees with Orazio Grassi on his interpretation of comets in *Discourse on the Comets*.

1619

Grassi and his colleagues write *The Astronomical and Philosophical Balance*, criticizing Galileo's views.

1623

Galileo publishes *The Assayer*, in reply to Grassi's criticisms, arguing for a moving Earth.

1624

Galileo is invited to Rome by Pope Urban VIII.
Agrees to write a book discussing alternative theories of the universe.
Starts to write *Dialogue Concerning the Two Chief Systems of the World*.

1632

Galileo publishes *Dialogue Concerning the Two Chief Systems of the World* and is summoned to Rome.

1633

Galileo is examined by the Inquisition and condemned to life imprisonment.

1634

Galileo's daughter, Virginia, dies.

1637

Galileo goes blind.

1638

Two New Sciences is smuggled out and published in Holland.

1639

Jeremiah Horrocks makes the first observations of the passage of Venus between the Sun and the Earth.

1641

Galileo devises the basis of the pendulum clock.

1642

8 January: Galileo dies.
December: Isaac Newton is born.

1649

Galileo's son, Vincenzio, dies.

1655

Christiaan Huygens patents the pendulum clock.

1659

Galileo's daughter, Livia, dies.

1687

Newton publishes laws of motion and gravitation.

1905

Albert Einstein publishes his special theory of relativity.

1969

Astronauts land on the Moon.

1992

Pope John Paul II publicly accepts Galileo's discoveries.

Glossary

Acceleration
Increase in speed. It was Galileo who clearly explained this concept.

Astronomy
The scientific study of objects beyond the Earth.

Atmosphere
The layer of gases surrounding the Earth or other planet or star.

Comet
Lump of ice, grit and dust which moves in a long path through the solar system. When comets approach the Sun, they form tails of gas and dust.

Density
The amount of material in a particular volume (such as a cubic centimetre) of a substance.

Dowry
The money given by the bride's family when she marries.

Experiment
A practical test of an idea.

Fifth essence
A mysterious substance believed by Aristotle to compose the Moon and everything beyond it. The other four essences were Earth, Water, Air and Fire.

Fresco
A type of painting made on damp, fresh plaster, on a wall or ceiling.

Gravity
The force that keeps people on the ground, makes stones fall to Earth and keeps the Moon orbiting the Earth and the planets orbiting the Sun.

Law of motion
Mathematical statements explaining the way objects move.

Magnetism
The property of some materials to attract iron and some other metals.

Mechanical clock
A device which tells the time by means of gear-wheels which are moved by the power of a falling weight or a spring.

Nuclear reactions
Energy released when the nucleus in an atom splits spontaneously or when it hits another particle.

Observation
To accurately watch and record.

Orbit
The path of one body around another in space.

Patron
A person who gives their financial support and approval to another person.

Projectile
An object that can be thrown, fired or shot.

Relativity
Principle that it makes no sense to state that an object moves, except in relation to another object.

Solar system
The Sun and the planets, moons, comets, meteoroids, dust and gases that surround it.

Sunspot
A dark area on the surface of the Sun.

Supernova
An explosion that increases the brightness of a star many millions of times.

Universe
Everything that exists.

Water clock
A device that measures time by recording the level of water either flowing out of or into it.

Further Information

Books for younger readers

Famous Lives: Scientists
by Nina Morgan (Wayland, 1993)

Galileo Galilei
by Michael White (Exley, 1991)

Groundbreakers: Galileo Galilei
by Paul Mason (Heinemann, 2000)

Heavens Above: The Story of Galileo Galilei
by Kenneth Ireland (Hodder Wayland, 1997)

Livewire Real Lives: Galileo
by Brandon Robshaw
(Hodder & Stoughton Educational, 1999)

Science Discoveries: Galileo and the Universe
by Steve Parker (Belitha, 1992)

Spinning through Space: The Solar System by Tim Furniss (Hodder Wayland, 2000)

Spinning through Space: The Sun
by Tim Furniss (Hodder Wayland, 2000)

Spinning through Space: Comets and Asteroids
by Eva M. Hans (Hodder Wayland, 2000)

Spinning through Space: Constellations
by Eva M. Hans (Hodder Wayland, 2000)

Spinning through Space: Space Travel
by Dr Mike Goldsmith (Hodder Wayland, 2000)

Spinning through Space: Space Mysteries
by Dr Mike Goldsmith (Hodder Wayland, 2000)

Books for older readers

The Ascent of Man
by Jacob Bronowski (BBC, 1988)

Galileo
by Colin Ronan
(Weidenfeld and Nicolson, 1974)

Websites

The Galileo Project, Rice University
http://es.rice.edu/ES/humsoc/Galileo
Information on the life and work of Galileo.

The Galileo Room, Institute and Museum of the History of Science of Florence, Italy
http://galileo.imss.firenze.it/museo/4

Index

Page numbers in **bold** are pages where there is a photograph or an illustration.